W9-CHH-307

Letters
FROM HEAVEN
REASSURING WORDS OF GOD'S LOVE

J. JAY SANDERS

BARBOUR
PUBLISHING, INC.

Imagine for a moment that your mailbox began to fill with letters from Heaven—from the very pen of God Himself. What would He say to you? *Scott – My Dear Scott*

Perhaps He would remind you of His everlasting love. . .of His power to help in your times of trouble. . .of His joy at your success and His pain in your failures. . .of His readiness to forgive.

In a very real sense, all Christians have received a letter from God—His Word, the Bible. This little book that you hold now serves to remind you of the reassuring thoughts God has for you in His "letter," the Bible. Think of Him as a loving Father, offering comforting words to you, His child. Find peace and encouragement in His *Letters from Heaven*. . .

I'm your Father, and I. . .

*A*ccept ~~you~~ Scott as
My unique creation.

~

God created ~~man~~ Scott in
His own image.
GENESIS 1:27

~

*We as Christians have
an image for
projection to the world.*

A. NAISMITH

I'm your Father, and I. . .

$\mathcal{B}$elieve ~~you are~~ *Scott is* precious and valuable.

~

The very hairs of your head
are all numbered.
So, do not fear;
Scott is ~~you are~~ more valuable
than many sparrows.
MATTHEW 10:30–31

I am the God of the stars.

Lift up thine eyes and see

As far as mortals may

Into eternity!

And stay thy heart on Me.

AMY CARMICHAEL

I'm your Father, and I. . .

*C*are about your hurts,
tears, and all that touches you.

~

Casting all your anxiety on Him,
because He cares for you,
1 PETER 5:7

~

Worry says,
" is a wimp."
Casting says,
"God is all powerful."

I'm your Father, and I. . .

$\mathcal{D}$esire only
what is best for ~~you.~~ *Scott*

~

"For I know the plans that I have for ~~you,~~ *Scott*"
declares the LORD,
"plans for welfare and not for calamity
to give ~~you~~ *Scott* a future and a hope."
JEREMIAH 29:11

~

I will fling open wide a door of hope,
And I will give ~~you~~ Scott back
Years that the locusts have devoured;
No good thing shall ~~you~~ Scott lack.
NANCY HANSEN

Letters FROM HEAVEN

I'm your Father, and I. . .

*E*stablish this promise.

~

The steps of a ~~man~~ Scat are
established by the LORD,
And He delights in his way.
When he falls,
he will not be hurled headlong,
Because the LORD is
the One who holds his hand.
PSALM 37:23–24

~

*No matter how
difficult the way
He promises to
hold ~~us~~ steady.*

~

I'm your Father, and I. . .

 *F*orgive all ~~your~~ *Scott* sins,
even future ones
yet uncommitted.

~

"Behold,
the Lamb of God who
takes away the sin of the world!"
JOHN 1:29

~

The cross crosses out

ALL ~~my~~ *Scott's* *sin.*

I'm your Father, and I. . .

*G*ive the Holy Spirit to
assist ~~you~~ *Scott* with your prayers.

~

In the same way
the Spirit also helps our weakness;
for we do not know
how to pray as we should,
but the Spirit Himself intercedes for ~~us~~ *Scott*
with groanings too deep for words.
ROMANS 8:26

~

*When we pray
it is as a duet,
not a solo.*

I'm your Father, and I. . .

Have no intentions
of leaving or
rejecting you. *Scott*

~

"I will be with you; *Scott*
I will not fail you or forsake you. *Scott*
JOSHUA 1:5

And none shall pluck us
from that hand.
Eternally ~~we are~~ *Scott is* secure.
Though heaven and earth
shall pass away,
His word forever shall endure.

MRS. M. E. RAE

I'm your Father, and I. . .

*I*nvite ~~you~~ Scott to let Me
into your heart.

~

"Behold, I stand at the door and knock;
if anyone hears My voice and opens the door,
I will come in to him and will dine with him,
and he with Me."
REVELATION 3:20

~

This place is occupied.
DR. F. W. BOREHAM

I'm your Father, and I. . .

*J*ust want ~~you~~ *Scott* to know
that I love ~~you~~ *Scott.*

~

"The LORD your God is in ~~your~~ *Scott's* midst,
A victorious warrior.
He will exult over ~~you~~ *Scott* with joy,
He will be quiet in His love,
He will rejoice over ~~you~~ *Scott* with shouts of joy."
ZEPHANIAH 3:17

~

Love bore our sins away;
Love gave us life anew;
Love opened wide the gates of heaven;
Love gave us work to do.
RUTH A. ATWELL

I'm your Father, and I. . .

$\mathcal{K}$eep a protective eye
on you.

~

For he who touches ~~you~~, Scott
touches the apple of His eye.
ZECHARIAH 2:8

~

Jehovah-Sabaoth
encamps around
His children.

~

I'm your Father, and I. . .

*L*ove ~~you.~~ Scott
One can never say
those words enough.

~

Walk in love,
just as Christ also loved ~~you~~ Scott
and gave Himself up for ~~us.~~ Scott
EPHESIANS 5:2

~

Lord, help ~~me~~ Scott over life's rough road
To share my brother's heavy load.
Since Christ bore mine for me.
S. E. BURROW

I'm your Father, and I. . .

$\mathcal{M}$arvel at how ~~you~~ Scott
have grown and changed.

~

Grow in the grace and knowledge
of our Lord and Savior Jesus Christ.
2 PETER 3:18

~

Though I am not what I ought to be,
nor what I wish to be,
nor yet hope to be, I can
truly say I am not what I once was,
a slave to sin and Satan.
JOHN NEWTON

I'm your Father, and I. . .

*N*ever ignore
your Advocate.

~

My little children,
I am writing these things to ~~you~~ *Scott*
so that you may not sin.
And if anyone sins,
we have an Advocate with the Father,
Jesus Christ the righteous.
1 JOHN 2:1

Christ's work as Advocate comes into operation as soon as we sin. . . . We have a lovely word in Africa used to express this idea. An advocate or comforter is sometimes called a "kasendo mukwashi." The first word, "kasendo," means "a blood brother," one with whom a solemn covenant sealed in blood has been made. The second word, "mukwashi," means "one who helps by laying hold." The Lord is both to us.

T. ERNEST WILSON

I'm your Father, and I. . .

*O*ffered My son so
that we could be
together forever.

~

For God so loved the world,
that He gave His only begotten Son,
that whoever believes in Him
shall not perish,
but have eternal life.
JOHN 3:16

~

Enough said.

I'm your Father, and I. . .

*P*raise your achievements both small and great.

~

Let another praise ~~you,~~ Scott
and not your own mouth.
PROVERBS 27:2

~

Surpassing all other honors

is the King's,

"Well done!"

DR. NORTHCOTE DECK

I'm your Father, and I. . .

*Q*uickly run to ~~your~~ Scott's aid
anytime, anywhere.

~

For you were continually straying like sheep,
but now you have returned to
the Shepherd and Guardian of your souls.
1 PETER 2:25

In the town of Woeden in Germany,
on the tower of a fine church building
is the carved figure of a lamb.
It was placed there to
commemorate the remarkable escape
from death of a workman who fell
from the high scaffolding when
the tower was being built.
At the moment of his fall a flock of
sheep was being driven by,
and he had fallen on one of the lambs,
which was crushed to death.
The carved figure of the lamb
was placed there to commemorate the
incident, and also to remind all
who came that way of the Lamb
of God who died to save sinners.

A. NAISMITH

Letters FROM HEAVEN

I'm your Father, and I. . .

*R*ejoice over
our friendship.

~

Greater love
has no one than this,
that one lay down his life
for his friends.
JOHN 15:13

What a friend we have in Jesus,
All our sins and griefs to bear.
What a privilege to carry
Everything to God in prayer.

JOSEPH SCRIVEN

Letters FROM HEAVEN

I'm your Father, and I. . .

See every moment
of ~~your~~ Scott's life.

~

O LORD,
You have searched me and known me.
You know when I sit down
and when I rise up;
You understand my thought from afar.
You scrutinize my path and my lying down,
And are intimately acquainted
with all my ways.
Even before there is a word on my tongue,
Behold, O LORD, You know it all.
PSALM 139: 1–4

We're in His hand,
that mighty Hand
That flung a universe in space,
That guides the sun
and the moon and stars
And holds the planets
in their place.

MRS. M. E. RAE

I'm your Father, and I. . .

Tell ~~Scott~~ ~~you~~ that
My eyes search for ~~you~~ ~~Scott~~.

~

For the eyes of the LORD move
to and fro throughout the earth
that He may strongly support
those whose heart is completely His.
2 CHRONICLES 16:9

~

He intently looks for
those intent on being
totally surrendered to
His Lordship.

I'm your Father, and I. . .

*U*nderstand
~~your~~ Scott's weaknesses.

~

For we do not have a high priest who cannot
sympathize with our weaknesses,
but One who has been tempted
in all things as we are,
yet without sin.
HEBREWS 4:15

~

Jesus loves me this I know,
For the Bible tells me so.
Little ones to Him belong—
They are weak but He is strong.
WILLIAM BRADBURY

I'm your Father, and I. . .

Value you. ~~Scott~~

~

So, do not fear;
~~Scott~~ you are more valuable
than many sparrows.
MATTHEW 10:31

~

*Nobody knows
what a human is worth.
How do you put
a price tag on the cross?*

~

I'm your Father, and I. . .

*W*alk ~~you~~ *Scott* through
the dark times.

~

Even though I walk through
the valley of the shadow of death,
I fear no evil,
for You are with me.
PSALM 23:4

~

Confidence—
"I will fear no evil."

H. A. IRONSIDE

I'm your Father, and I give you. . .

$\mathcal{X}$(Christos),
anointing your life with
My power.

~

You prepare a table before me *Scott*
in the presence of my *Scott's* enemies;
You have anointed
Scott's my head with oil.
PSALM 23:5

~

*Anointed sheep
do not fear an unanointed enemy.*

I'm your Father, and I. . .

*Y*earn to have
fellowship with ~~you.~~ Scott
today + always

What we have seen and heard
we proclaim to you also,
so that you too may have
fellowship with us;
and indeed our fellowship is
with the Father,
and with His Son Jesus Christ.
1 JOHN 1:3

To walk with God—
'tis not too late to join
That holy band
who soared above the sod
Of transient things,
of weights, besetting sins,
And feel the mighty pulse
of life with God.

JBN

I'm your Father, and I. . .

*Z*ealously look to the day
that ~~you~~ *Scott* come home
to be with Me.

~

"If I go and prepare a place for ~~you~~, *Scott*
I will come again and receive ~~you~~ *Scott* to Myself,
that where I am, there ~~you~~ *Scott* may be also."
JOHN 14:3

~

"To Christians heaven is
their everlasting home.
The most marvelous thing about it is
that God has prepared it
for those who love Him."

MATTHEW HENRY